Fun with Physics

COLIN SIDDONS

line drawings by David Armitage

KAYE & WARD · LONDON
in association with Methuen of Australia
and Hicks, Smith, New Zealand

Contents

First published by Kaye & Ward Ltd
21 New Street, London EC2M 4NT
1978

Copyright © 1978 Kaye & Ward Ltd

ISBN 0 7182 1313 0

Set in VIP Palatino by Bishopsgate Press Ltd,
London
Printed in Great Britain by Cox & Wyman Ltd,
London, Fakenham and Reading

Foreword

Modern Physics is a very large-scale subject. Particle Generators, for example, are huge in size, highly complex and very expensive. To use them requires large teams of scientists, engineers and mathematicians.

The experiments described in this book, on the other hand, are small, simple and cheap. Most of the pieces of apparatus are to be home-made. Some of them require items such as copper wire which is relatively cheap but not easily bought; perhaps a friendly science teacher will help you here.

Some of the experiments are with objects such as Slinkie, i.e. scientific toys which are not expensive and easily obtained. Two toys, however, the Hot Air Engine and Radio Rex, are no longer available. I have included these because they make, I think, interesting reading.

I have enjoyed trying out the experiments described in this book: may you too have pleasure in repeating, modifying and even improving them!

Fun with Water

Floating

Real floaters

Everybody knows that wooden blocks and corks float on water. Other objects to try are:

    ping-pong balls
    candles
    ice-cubes
    empty containers rescued from the kitchen scrap-bin.

To make a floating platform glue three empty cartons or three ping-pong balls to a triangular piece of cardboard as shown in diagram 1. On these platforms you can erect a long thin piece of wood bearing a flag.

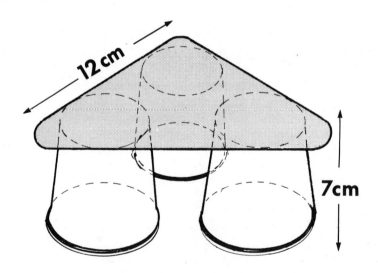

1   A floating platform

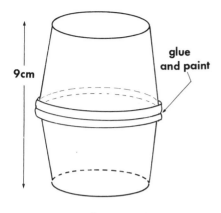

glue
and paint

9cm

2   A floating vessel

Both-way floaters

An empty custard powder tin with lid replaced can float in two different ways: it will float with its axis horizontal and it will float with its axis vertical.

Fasten together, with adhesive or with paint, two empty plastic salad containers as shown in diagram 2. You will probably find that the combined vessel will float both ways. Make a collection of such two-way floaters. The best one I have is made from two cups of expanded polystyrene as shown in the photo. Only $1/80$th part of the volume of the floater is beneath the surface and yet it will float upright quite steadily.

A good floater

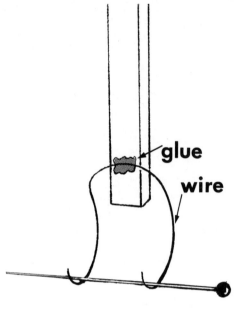

3　Launching a pin

Maybe floaters

Wooden blocks and corks are real floaters: if you push them beneath the surface of the water and then let go they come up again with a rush.

There are a number of objects however which will float if they are carefully placed on the surface, but once pushed through the surface sink and remain sunk. These objects we will call 'maybe floaters'.

(i) Pins and needles. To begin with, try safety pins and paper clips. It is easy to float these. Then go on to pins and needles. The launcher shown in diagram 3 is a great help here. The pin, resting in the launcher, is carefully lowered onto the surface of the water: the launcher is then carefully removed. From thin pins go on to thicker needles. Two tips are helpful here:

1. Wipe the water surface clean with a strip of newspaper
2. Put a little grease (vaseline) on the ends of the needle.

Modern knitting needles, though they look like plastic, are made of aluminium. With a hacksaw, cut a short length (2 or 3 inches) from a No. 10 knitting needle. You should be able to float this with the help of the launcher. Thicker needles have smaller gauge numbers. I have never been able to float needles that were thicker than No. 10s.

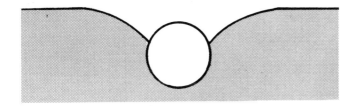

4 Floating needle

Float the needle in a transparent vessel e.g. a rectangular sandwich box. Look at the needle first from the top. You will see the water curving *down* to the needle. Then look from the side. The needle is *below* the surface of the water. Diagram 4 shows a cross section of the floating pin.

Water behaves as if there were — there is not really — a kind of skin on its surface, keeping the water together. In the surface there is a pulling force, a tension. This 'surface tension' in water and other liquids is of the greatest importance in understanding them. It is this tension which supports the pins and needles.

When you have a No. 10 needle floating on water rub a finger on your forehead and dip it in the water near the needle. The needle should move sharply away and then sink. The grease (sebum) from your forehead has weakened the surface tension and so the water surface is no longer strong enough to support the needle.

(ii) Tin lids. Tins of course are not made of tin but of steel plate. The lids of tin cans are generally not quite flat, the flattest being those of coffee-tins. Such lids float easily on water, thanks to surface tension. Not only do they float but they will take a load. A thin wooden rod can be stuck to the middle by plasticine or Blue-Tak. It is very interesting to watch the wall of water round the edge of the lid as the load is increased. It gets to be about 3 mm high before eventually sinking occurs.

If the floating lid is illuminated by a lamp from above, its shadow on the bottom of the vessel has a bright ring around it. When you have a lid floating in water touch the water with a rod which has been dipped in soapy water. The lid will sink; soap reduces the surface tension of water; that is why we use soap for washing.

(iii) Another maybe floater is a sieve. We require a small plastic sieve, about 6 cm in diameter such as is sold in hardware shops for use in the kitchen. The mesh is made up of nylon fibres. The square holes in such a sieve have sides a little less than 1 mm in length. Cut off the plastic handle

5   But it holds water!

and you will then find that the sieve floats quite happily. The surface tension of the water holds it back from passing through the fine holes of the sieve.

Sieves, too, though full of holes, will hold water but not a great deal. Besides plastic sieves the metal sieves used as tea or coffee strainers will do. Pour water into such a sieve very gently. You will be surprised how much water it holds before leaking begins. If you touch the underside of the sieve before it has started to leak you will find that leakage will then begin. Campers know very well that they must not touch the underside of the canvas roof of the tent on rainy days.

Transparent plastic cups rescued from the kitchen scrap bin enable us to make something like sieves. With a hand-drill bore a hole $1/16$th inch in the side of such a cup near the bottom. Pour water in very gently. Measure how high the water can be above the hole before leaking takes place — I find that it can be as high as 15 mm. Finer holes, $1/32$ and $1/64$ inch can be made but the drills have to be held in a pin vice. With $1/64$ inch holes I find that leaking does not start until the head of water is 4 cm.

With the finest drill that you have make 20 or more holes in the base of a plastic cup — then tell a friend that you a have a cup full of holes that can hold water (diagram 5).

Air and water: in and out

Tin cans

For this experiment you need a can with a tight-fitting lid such as a treacle tin. Hammer a hole in the middle of the base. Block this hole with your finger, fill the can with water and put the lid on firmly. Lift the can up. Water will not flow *out* because air cannot get *in*. (You can, however, get the water out by vigorous shaking).

Make two holes in the base of a second can as far apart as possible. Fill it with water. Hold it up straight. Nothing happens. Tilt it a little: water will begin to flow *out* of the lower hole because air, being lighter, will now go *in* at the higher hole (diagram 6) gurgling as it does so.

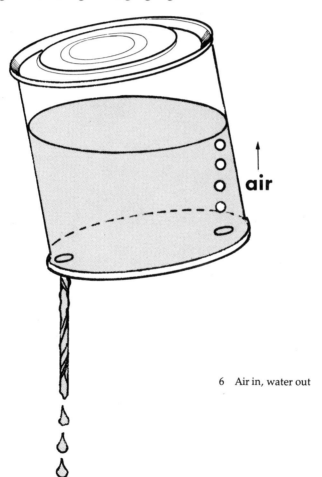

6   Air in, water out

9

Detergent bottles

It is easy to drill holes in detergent bottles since they are made of soft plastic, polythene. These bottles too, unlike tin cans, can be squeezed inwards. Bore eight small holes round the bottom edge of a detergent bottle, making sure that all the holes are at the same height. Fill the bottle with water. Replace the stopper. As long as the bottle is held upright nothing happens, but on tilting water will flow out of the lower holes.

Next hold the bottle full of water up and tell a friend that you have a bottle full of water and full of holes. If your friend does not believe you, squeeze the bottle — eight streams of water will shoot out (diagram 7).

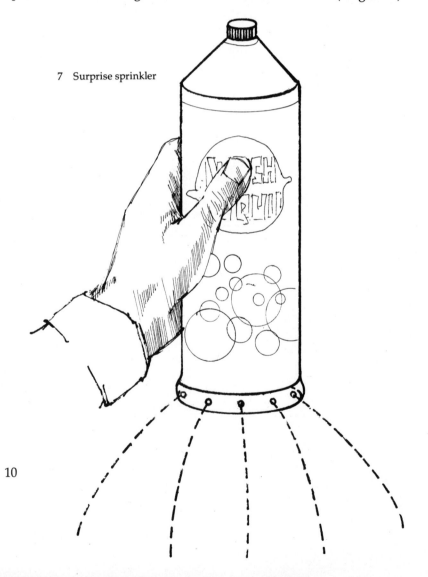

7 Surprise sprinkler

Sponges

For this experiment a big sponge is required: rectangular sponges sold for cleaning cars are suitable e.g. those of dimensions 20 × 13 × 5½ cm. Hold such a sponge under water until it is saturated. Bring it out. Hold it on two rulers so that its big faces are horizontal. No water will flow out. Lower one of the rulers. Water will then flow out of the lowest edge of the sponge.

What was true for the tin can with two holes and for the bottle with eight holes is still true for the sponge with hundreds if not thousands of holes: if air cannot get *in* water cannot get *out*.

The beaker and card

Fill a beaker, a transparent plastic one preferably, with water. Lay a piece of cardboard on top: the cardboard must completely cover the surface of the water. Hold the cardboard firmly in place and then turn the beaker over. The card will stay put. Once again water cannot get out because air cannot get in. Try again with the beaker only half full of water. (See diagram 8.) What happens now? Make a small hole in the centre of the card before putting it in its place. What happens?

Plastic beakers are about 7½ cm deep and 7 cm broad. Try with bigger vessels. Suitable ones are: jam jars (12 × 5 cm), coffee tins (7½ × 10 cm), tin cans (11½ × 7½ cm). You should have no difficulty with these, the water should stay in. If you try bigger vessels still, do so out-of-doors so that if there is a flood it does no harm.

8 Beaker and card

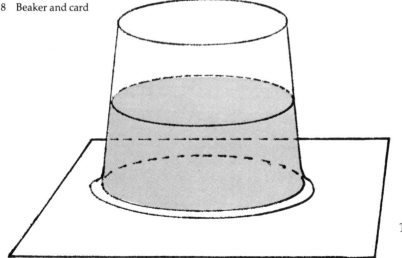

11

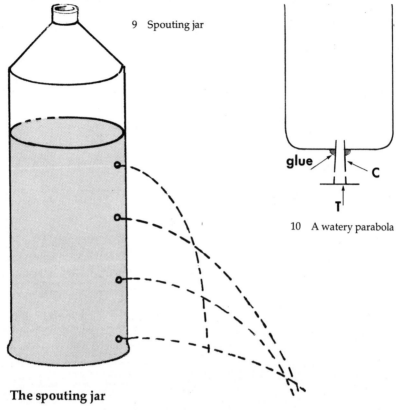

9 Spouting jar

10 A watery parabola

The spouting jar

Bore four small holes, one above the other, in the side of a detergent bottle. Fill the bottle with water. Water spouts out of the holes as shown (diagram 9). Near the top of the water the pressure is small so the water is not pushed out strongly through the top hole. As we go down in the water the pressure increases, the water is pushed out more vigorously and the water jets spread more.

A watery parabola

The shape of the water jets from the holes in the spouting jar is called, by mathematicians, a 'parabola'. We can make a double-sided parabola as follows: (see diagram 10)

C is a slightly tapering tube. I made one by cutting a suitable section from a discarded ball-point pen with a hack-saw. There are two small holes in it near the base, made with a $1/16$ inch drill. The end is sealed off by glueing a piece of tin-plate (T) to it.

To make a hole in the bottom of the detergent bottle big enough to take the tube, bore a small hole with a drill and then enlarge it by twisting the blade of a pen-knife in it, testing from time to time until the tube can just be pushed in. It is then glued to make it water-tight.

Again this is an out-of-doors experiment for the water jets can go quite considerable distances.

As the photo shows, soon after leaving the holes, each jet breaks up into two or three jets. When there is a lot of water in the bottle the pressure is high and the parabola is a wide one, but as the water runs out the pressure becomes less and the parabola becomes narrower.

A parabola is really quite a common shape: when an object such as a cricket ball is thrown through the air its path is a parabola.

A watery parabola

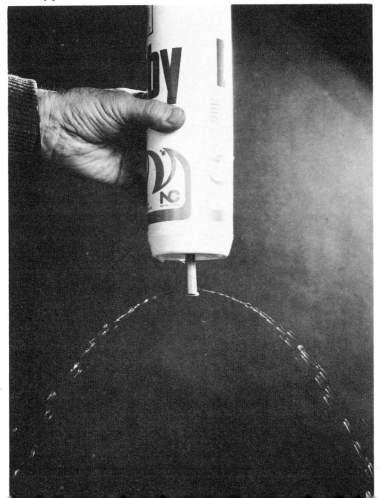

13

Flowing uphill

Diagram 11 shows a siphon at work. As long as the level of the water in container B is above that in A, water will flow up the tube so that B empties and A fills up. Water will flow up one side of the tube provided that it can flow a bigger distance down the other side of the tube. The bigger the difference in the two water levels the faster the flow. When the two levels are nearly equal the flow becomes very slow.

To start the siphon working the tube must be filled with water. One way of doing this is to suck the air out of one end of the tube whilst the other end is under water.

For A and B use transparent vessels e.g. jam jars. For the tube either plastic ones or rubber ones can be used. Narrow plastic tubes can be bought in model shops. The wider the tube the faster the flow and the sooner the two levels become equal.

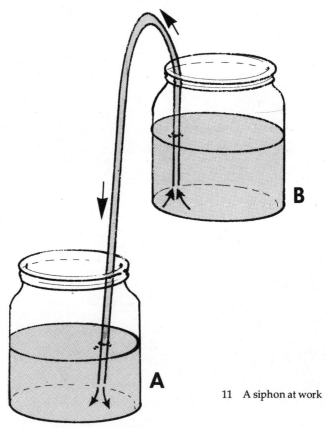

B

A

11   A siphon at work

14

Creeping uphill

Cut a strip from a paper towel or hankie about 20 cm long and 2 or 3 cm wide. Fasten it to a suitable support at the top and allow the bottom end to dip into water in a basin. The paper at the bottom becomes darker as the water creeps up it. I found that in the first minute it rose up 4 cm but after that it rose at a slower rate and would not go up much more than about 10 cm however long I left it.

If you examine a paper towel you will find that it consists of two thin sheets pressed together. There are, however, air spaces between the sheets. Water flows up narrow spaces or tubes by the 'capillary effect'. The usefulness of paper towels, their ability to mop up water, depends upon this capillary effect.

Similarly if a dry sponge is held with its bottom end in water, after a time water will have moved into the sponge.

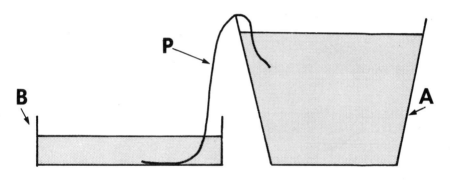

12   A paper siphon

Siphons

A paper siphon

With a paper towel we can combine the siphon and capillary effects. Diagram 12 shows a length of paper towel P cut into a strip with its top end dipping into water in a transparent vessel A. (A round vessel will do but there is an advantage in using one with straight sides.)

The bottom end rests in a container B. Water rises up the towel over the rim of A and then down into B where it flows out. If a double thickness is used the rate of flow is increased.

15

The rate of flow of this paper siphon depends upon the height the water has to rise from the surface in A to the rim. When A is full the rate of flow is quick, the level in A in consequence falls, the water has a greater height to rise to get over the rim and so the flow slows down.

You may at one time have left an ordinary towel with one end in water in a wash basin or bowl, the other hanging over the edge. You will be able to understand now why the towel got so wet.

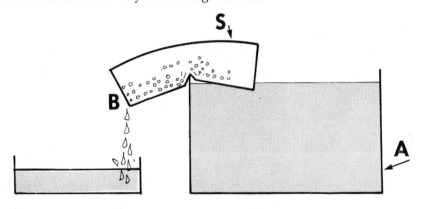

13   A sponge siphon

A sponge siphon

A is a square vessel e.g. a plastic cake container. (See diagram 13). The bottom half of the sponge S is wetted and then the sponge is balanced on the rim of A as shown. Water will pour out rapidly from the edge B of the sponge. As with the paper towel experiment we have here a combination of the siphon and the capillary effects. When the edge B becomes equal in height to the level of the water in A, the flow stops.

A trick jug

On holiday in Italy I found, in a gift shop, a toy which I had sought in vain in England — a trick jug. Noblemen used to amuse themselves and their guests with such jugs. Round the rim are the words BEVI SE PUOI which means 'Drink if you can'. (See diagram 14).

There are six large holes in the neck of the jug. The nobleman would pour wine into the jug and challenge any of his guests to drink the wine without spilling a drop. A smart guest would guess that the rim and handle were hollow and that therefore if he sucked at the spout he would

16

get the wine — and win the wager. However when he sucked he would be disappointed: he would hear a gurgling noise but he would get no wine. Then the nobleman would lift the jug and drain it at one go.

His secret was simple. Underneath the handle, out of sight near the top, is a hole. When he lifted the jug he would cover this hole with a finger, at the same time diverting the onlookers attention elsewhere. Now when he sucked he would lower the pressure of the air in the handle. The atmospheric pressure on the surface of the wine would send it up the handle, round the rim, through the spout and into his throat.

These jugs are interesting examples of the potter's art. How is the rim and handle made hollow? The answer is given below.

the hole

14   Drink — if you can!

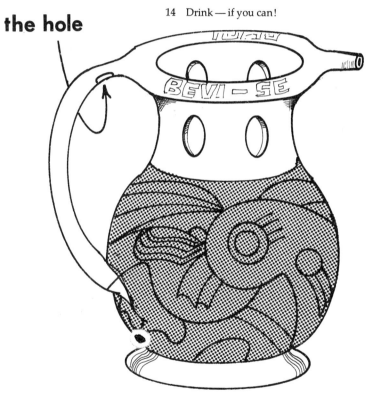

Answer When the clay is moulded to form the jug a piece of string forms the centre piece of the handle and rim. This burns away to nothing when the jug is fired in the kiln.

The diver in the bottle

There is a well-known toy in which a small diver floats in water in a bottle. When the cork is pushed in further or, in some cases, when the sides of the bottle are squeezed the diver sinks to the bottom. On releasing the pressure the diver comes to the top again. The diver is hollow — his inside is full of air. There is a hole in his base.

When the pressure on the diver is increased the air is compressed and a little water enters the diver. This makes the diver denser, denser in fact than the water, and so he sinks. When the pressure is released the air expands and pushes water out to lower the density of the diver and so bring him to the top again.

Do-it-yourself Cartesian diver

To make your own 'Cartesian' diver, as he is called, you need two transparent tubes, one long and wide, the other short and narrow. The

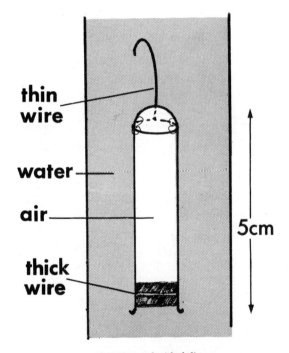

15   The undecided diver

second one is to float upside down in water contained in the first. For the wider tube I have used a plastic one 30 cm long and 2½ cm in diameter, which I bought at Easter time when it was filled with chocolate eggs. For the smaller tube I used a test-tube 5 cm long, 7 mm in diameter, such as are provided in Chemistry sets.

A thin wire ending in a hook is wrapped round and glued to the closed end of the tube as shown in diagram 15. The open end of the tube is loaded with thick copper wire, the length of which is adjusted until the tube floats with only the tip of the hook showing. A little patience is required here.

The diver is now launched. Using a long, thin rod with a suitable end-piece, the diver is pushed down a short distance and then released. If he comes up, push him down a little further until eventually when he is let go he does not know whether to go up or down. This is the critical position — if he is released from a point above this he floats up, from a point below this then he sinks down. At the critical position the density of the diver just equals the density of water.

To retrieve the diver when he has sunk to the bottom the long rod is used again. A hook is fastened to its end — this hook is made to catch the hook on the diver and then the latter is fished out.

If a longer tube e.g. one 50 cm or more, is available the adjustment of the wire is not so difficult and more fun can be had.

The camphor duck

The camphor duck is another well-known toy. When it works — it doesn't always — it swims around majestically in a large dish filled with water. It is made of plastic and about 2 cm long. Small lumps of camphor are pushed into a cleft in its tail.

The secret of making it work is quite simple. The surface of the water must be quite free from oil. To make it so, pull a strip of paper across the surface, cut off the wet edge of the paper and repeat this two or three times. Once the water has been cleaned keep your fingers out of it.

Camphor, like a number of other substances, lowers the surface tension of water. The camphor is at the back of the duck and so the tension pulling the duck backwards is less than the tension of the clean water at the front pulling the duck forwards — so the duck moves forwards.

19

Why has it to be camphor, why will not other substances do? The camphor forms a very thin layer on the water and this quickly evaporates thus leaving the surface quite clean again. The ability of camphor to evaporate is shown by its strong smell: if you leave small flakes of camphor on a sheet of paper overnight, next morning they will all have gone.

Make your own camphor boats

It is a simple matter to make, if not a camphor duck, all manner of camphor sailing craft. Camphor blocks can be bought for a few pennies at the chemist's — their smell is that of well-known ointments.

As we have already seen, the lids of 'tin' cans, though of steel, are thin enough to float on water. (The flat tops of coffee tins are suitable). These lids can be cut with strong scissors e.g. gardening scissors, into suitable shapes. Three such shapes are shown in diagrams 16A and B. A short length of drinking straw, preferably a plastic one, glued to the centre not only serves as a mast but also allows you to launch the vessel without touching the water.

From a block of camphor cut off a few flakes with a pen-knife and then make a small pile of them. Fix small lumps of blue-tak at the appropriate places on the edge of the metal, then push the blue-tak into the pile of flakes — in this way the camphor flakes are fastened to the boat.

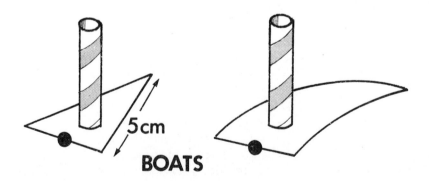

BOATS

16A   Camphor boats

Besides boats, which need a fairly large dish to move about in, you can make a rotor as shown in the diagram. All this needs is a small saucer. Rotors will rotate for hours without stopping. Larger ones turn round in a slow, stately way: little ones, e.g. 2 cm by 6 mm, whizz around. They rotate quickly enough in cold water; in warm water they spin round so quickly that it is hard to time them.

If you want to stop a camphor vessel moving, wipe a finger on your forehead and then dip it in the water. The vessel will immediately come to rest.

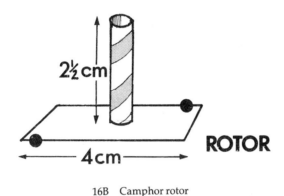

16B   Camphor rotor

Fun with Gravity

The falling pound

Hold a pound note up by its top edge. Ask a friend, especially one who considers himself quick off the mark, to hold his thumb and fore-finger near the bottom edge, ready to catch the note, as shown in diagram 17. He must not touch the note. Tell him that you are going to let go of the note without telling him when and that he has to try to catch it.

Generally he will not succeed. A few people however, those who have very quick re-actions, may do so. It is therefore not safe to say that if the note is caught it can be kept.

21

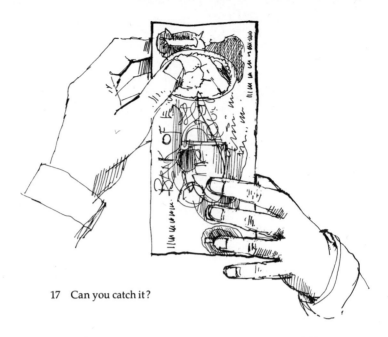

17 Can you catch it?

As soon as the note is let go it not only begins to fall, it begins to accelerate. Knowing the acceleration due to gravity we can calculate the time taken for a pound note which is just 6 inches long to fall its own length. This time is 0·18 seconds, (i.e. a little less than $1/5$th).

To catch the note therefore your friend in this time must have been able to:

        i)   pass information from eye to brain
        ii)   pass information from brain to hand
        iii)   to move the hand muscles the required distance.

Of course you do not need to use a pound note for this experiment. It is interesting indeed to use a series of cards of increasing length. The table gives the time taken by such cards to fall their own length:

Length of card (cm)	8	12	16	20
Time taken (seconds)	0·13	0·16	0·18	0·20

The next four toys, the woodpecker, the waddling ducks, the roley-poley and slinkie are all lifted up to begin with and so given energy, (potential energy). As they move downwards this energy is used up to keep the woodpecker pecking, the ducks waddling, the roly-poly rolling and the slinkie somersaulting.

22

The woodpecker pecks away

The woodpecker toy was on sale some time ago: it does not seem to be available now but it is a simple matter to make one.

The woodpecker is connected by a short spring to a block of wood B having a cylindrical hole of diameter slightly greater than that of the rod R (see diagram 18).

If the woodpecker is at rest, its weight tilts B so that the block remains fixed. If, whilst B is held, the woodpecker is set vibrating, the vibrations soon die down. But if the woodpecker is set vibrating whilst B is free, the vibrations continue, the bird pecks away at the rod, slowly falling all the time.

18   Pecking woodpecker

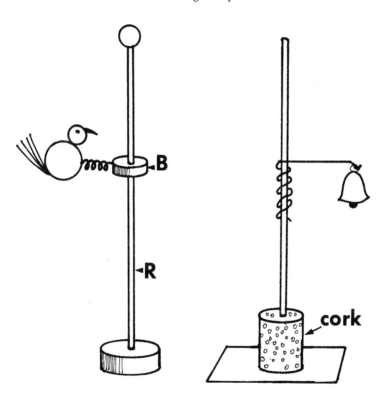

At the mid-point of each vibration B is vertical: it then slips a little way down R. This slight drop gives a jolt to the bird sufficient to keep it vibrating. At each drop, the energy of the bird due to its position, potential energy, is converted into energy of movement, kinetic energy.

The toy illustrates the basic idea of a grandfather clock. Once a fortnight grandfather hoisted up two great lead cylinders. The fall of these weights in a series of small steps provided the energy to keep the pendulum swinging.

To make a simpler version of this already simple toy you need first a long rod — it can be either a ½ cm wooden dowel or a long steel rod such as is sold in model shops. Twist a length of iron wire, or plastic coated copper wire, round the rod so that it fits loosely but not too loosely. The horizontal part of this wire provides the springiness. A little trial and error is required to get the right length. The end of the wire can carry a feather, a clothes peg or, as in diagram 18, a tinkling bell.

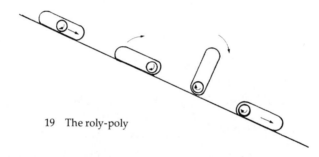

19   The roly-poly

Waddling ducks, roly-poly

Street salesmen sometimes sell little plastic ducks (or dogs, or soldiers) which when placed on a gentle slope walk down in a waddling kind of way. Some patience is required to get them to walk; the slope must not be too great, the surface must be neither too rough nor too smooth. When they do walk they are amusingly life-like.

It is not at all easy to explain why these ducks waddle rather than slide but it is easy to explain why another toy, which I will call a roly-poly, topples down a slope the way it does.

It consists of a cylindrical tube about 3 cm long inside which is a heavy ball (see diagram 19). When the tube is placed lengthways on a slope the ball inside rolls down and gathers a rolling speed ('rotational energy') as shown. When it hits the bottom end of the tube it communicates some of

24

this rotational energy to the tube which then does a somersault. Thus the tube rolls in its own peculiar jerky way down the slope.

Slinkie

This toy can be bought in toy-shops, especially educational-toy shops. My slinkie is a helix (spiral) and has 90 turns of diameter 7½ cm. At rest the turns sit loosely one on top of the other.

Walking downhill

The most amusing thing to do with slinkie is to get it to walk down a staircase. Hold one end against the top step, the bottom end against the next step down. Release both ends at the same time. Slinkie works its way down the stairs, the top end swinging over to become the bottom end which then finds its way in a surprisingly life-like fashion to the edge of the next step, the whole process then being repeated.

If steps are not available, slinkie will walk down a sloping plank as in the photo. Once again slinkie is an example of the potential energy of a body moving downhill being used, not to make it go faster, but to keep up another kind of movement.

The things we have experimented with so far, from pound-notes to Slinkie, all fall down and having fallen down, stay down. Now we are going to experiment with things that having fallen down manage to get up again. We can call these up-and-down toys though it would be more accurate to call them down-and-up ones.

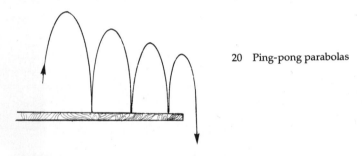

20   Ping-pong parabolas

Up and Down

The Ping-pong ball

Drop a ping-pong ball onto a hard surface such as a table top. It bounces up again after the collision but does not quite reach the height from which it started: some energy is lost in pushing the air out of the way, some is lost in making the 'ping'.

When I dropped a ball one metre, it bounced back about 90 cm the first time, then 81 cm the second time, each successive height being about $9/10$ths of the previous one. If the ball is thrown a little to one side, the path it takes is as shown in diagram 20, each of the curves being a parabola.

If you drop a ball onto a table and listen you will notice that the successive pings are nearer together in time, eventually becoming a continual sound whose pitch rises. You will notice, too, that the sound although it becomes weaker does not fade away: it stops at a quite definite and measurable moment. Thus when I dropped a ball 50 cm the time between the first ping and the end was 7·0 seconds.

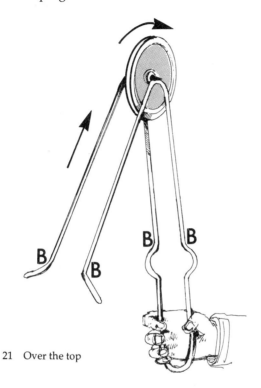

21   Over the top

The whirling wheel

This delightful toy is sometimes called a Magic Wheel but there is nothing magic about it at all. It works by a combination of gravity, rotational energy and magnetism.

As the wheel rolls downhill the gravitational energy it started with at the top is turned into rotational energy. The axle of the wheel has magnets at its ends and thus the axle is held firmly in contact with the steel rails. At the points B the axle slips from one side of the rails to the other side. (See diagram 21). The rotational energy of the wheel maintains the rolling and so it rolls back up near to its starting point. Some energy is lost in moving

27

through the air and so if the wheel is to be kept working, a little help has to be given to it i.e. some energy has to be added to it, to take it over the top. If it kept on rolling up and down without any assistance it really would be a magic wheel.

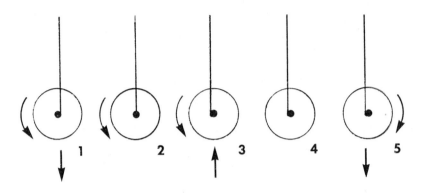

22 The movement of the yo-yo

The yo-yo

The well-known yo-yo is really very similar to the whirling wheel. In both a disc rolls down under the action of gravity and in so doing acquires a rotational energy which then takes it back up again: not quite all the way, so energy has to be fed in by the action of the hand to keep it going.

You may be quite satisfied just to work the yo-yo: this indeed is a great delight. If you are curious to know what happens, how a yo-yo works, consider diagram 22 which shows five successive positions of the disc.

In position 1 the disc is falling down and because the string is on the right of the axle, the disc is rotating in an anti-clockwise direction.

In position 2 the disc has reached the bottom of its path: the rotational energy of the disc keeps it rotating and so it rolls up the string as in position 3.

When the disc has used up all its rotational energy it is at the top of its upward journey — position 4. The string is now to the left of the axle so that when the disc falls this time it will rotate in a clockwise direction — position 5.

If you look at the disc as it falls and rises you will see, as the diagram explains, that every time the disc reaches the top of its path it changes its direction of rotation.

28

The skidding car

Sometimes unexpected things happen. To show a surprise skidding effect we need an inclined plane — e.g. a short, smooth plank — and a model car. First test that the car runs freely down the plane.

Next prevent the back wheels from turning e.g. tape them to the chassis. Put the car on the inclined plane. Most people expect that the car will proceed in a straight path down the plane, the back wheels skidding along. What happens is quite different: the car spins round so that the back wheels become the front ones and then it proceeds in a straight line down the plane.

If on the other hand you jam the front wheels, the car will move off in a straight line from the start. If you have two identical model cars jam the front wheels of one and the back wheels of the other. Then ask a friend which of the two will get to the bottom first if they are released at the same time side by side.

Falling through air

If objects are of compact shape and made of material of sufficiently high density when they fall they gather speed i.e. they accelerate. With such objects the resistance of the air is not important. Let us now drop some objects which, because of their shape, disturb a lot of air. The air therefore resists their fall and they do not accelerate but fall down at a steady speed.

First we use some objects provided by nature. Feathers are pleasant things to collect: you will soon find that different feathers fall in different ways. Fluffy curled feathers, on being dropped, float down gracefully with the concave side facing upwards: if you release them with the convex face upwards they turn over and then float down.

At different times of the year different 'slow-fallers' can be collected, e.g. dandelion parachutes, thistledown, the seeds of rosebay willow herb. When you have specimens of each, have a slow-fall competition. A launcher is useful for this purpose. Release the objects from a flat card fixed at right angles to the end of a long rod e.g. a garden cane.

Sycamore keys are well known. Flung up into the air, when they fall, they rotate at great speed and this slows down their fall.

From nature to man-made objects: some vegetables are sold in shallow trays made of a very light material, expanded polystyrene. If such a tray is dropped concave side facing upwards it falls steadily down, like the curly feathers we have mentioned. But if the concave side faces downwards it falls at first in an unruly way before it eventually turns over to fall concave side facing upwards.

You can make interesting 'slow-fallers' with tissue paper. The different ways that tissue paper shapes can fall down are numerous: keep an account showing the shape, size, whether the paper is flat or twisted, how it is released and then how it falls. Don't be surprised if you find that the same slow-faller falls in different ways at different times. The following gives a rough idea of what may happen:

i)   A tissue paper square, side 5 cm. This falls down in an unruly way but you will find that besides falling it swirls upwards as well

ii) A long, thin rectangle e.g. 6 cm × 2 mm. This can be made to fall either rotating rapidly about its long axis or slowly, like a helicopter, about an axis through its centre at right angles to its length

iii) Crosses. Make a cross by sticking together two rectangles each 5 cm × 2 mm. By giving a slight bend and a slight twist to each of its four arms this will helicopter down, falling slowly and steadily but rotating rapidly. When you have succeeded with a cross this size, try smaller ones and then bigger ones.

Fun with Soap Films

In the past, soap films really were made from soap and water: nowadays it is easier to make them with detergent and water. The name 'soap film' is still used however, it sounds better than 'detergent film'. I shall describe first some experiments with flat films and then some with bubbles. The length of life of soap films and bubbles depends upon the atmospheric conditions. In a warm, dry room, they may last only a few seconds: in a cold, damp place, e.g. a cellar, they will last three or four minutes.

A square film

A square frame of wooden rods or metal wires is required. The coat-hangers from dry cleaners are made of a soft metal. This is easily cut

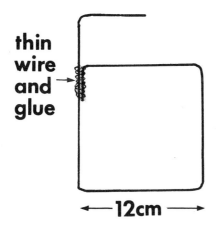

**thin
wire
and
glue** →

←—**12cm**—→

23   Frame for film

to the right length by a hack-saw. It can be bent to the correct shape by holding it in a vice. Make a square with handle as shown in diagram 23, the sides to be about 5 inches (12 cm).

The detergent solution has to be made in a flat container e.g. a roasting tin, big enough to dip the frame in. Fill the tin with water to the required depth and then add some detergent. Stir gently. Dip the frame in, withdraw it, look to see if a film is formed across the frame. If no film is formed add more detergent to the water until a good film is formed.

The films are not as fragile as you may think. If you gently shake the frame up and down the film will make quite big humps and hollows before it bursts.

They will also stand up to a lot of rough treatment by *wet* objects without bursting. Thus you can:

> poke a wet finger through the film
> push your wet hand through the film
> stab it with a wet knife
> bang it with a wet hammer.

Most surprising of all, a stream of water falling on the film will pass

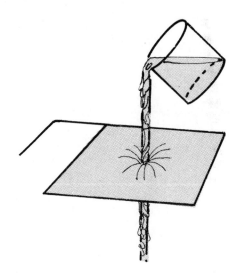

24   It doesn't burst!

through it, and the film will still be there (diagram 24).

You may ask: why is this possible? A short answer is that water does not repel water. A *dry* finger or a *dry* hammer will burst the film.

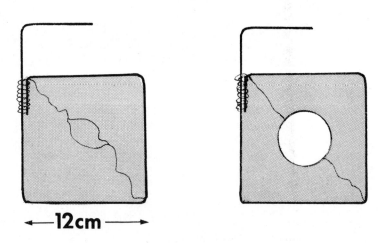

←—**12cm**—→

25   Surface tension

A circular hole

Fasten a length of thread with a loop in it from one corner of the frame to the opposite corner (see diagram 25). After immersion in the bucket the cotton will have no particular shape. Burst the film inside the loop. The loop now becomes a graceful circle.

This demonstrates neatly that soap films shrink as much as they can: in scientific language, they have the surface of minimum area. All liquids have this property but soap films show it most clearly.

You may find, if your fingers have become soapy, that they will not break the film, however hard you try. However, you can always burst the film with the hot end of an extinguished match.

Two needles

Take two long rods — knitting needles will do well — and fasten threads as shown. Dip in the tin and withdraw. At first hold the rods apart and then bring them nearer (see diagram 26). The film decreases, it seems to vanish. Separate the rods, you will find the film still there.

Hold the rods vertically. Move one of them up and down. The threads roll along each other in an amusing way.

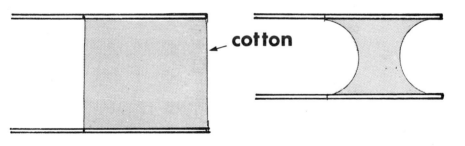

cotton

26   Two rods

The man in the moon

Make a wire curve W with a length of cotton A across it as shown, (diagram 27). When the pull in the thread B is relaxed the shape of the film is that of the crescent moon. Pull on B: we now get the shapes shown. Release B. The thread jumps back quickly to its first position.

27   The man in the moon

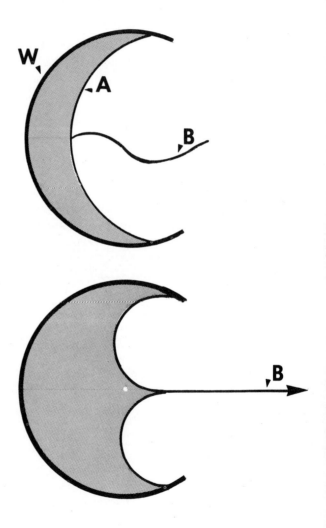

Fun with Bubbles

Spherical bubbles

To blow round bubbles we require a rubber tube and a small funnel. Dip the funnel into the soap solution and gently withdraw it. Blow down the rubber tube and you will get a bubble. Quite big ones can be blown this way. There are plenty of tricks and experiments that you can do with these bubbles.

They can be transferred from the funnel to the top of a beaker so that then your hands are free. Plastic tubs will serve as beakers. Their rims must be wetted before trying to transfer the bubble.

Blow two such bubbles and put them alongside each other (diagram 28). You can then have a boxing match, using one bubble to hit the other bubble with. At first they simply bounce off each other but eventually you will find that they stick together; the two 'boxers' have clinched.

Allow a spherical bubble resting on a cup to stand. Look at it from time to time. After a minute or two you will notice colours beginning to form near the top of the bubble. At first they swirl about in a restless motion but

28   Boxing bubbles

29   Coloured rings

then they settle down and brightly coloured rings can be seen (diagram 29). Watch the very centre of these rings carefully. Eventually a black dot, no bigger than a pin-head, appears but it soon grows and continues to grow. The film is now getting very thin, it will not last long. Sometimes the black area extends over as much as half the bubble. If you look from the side you see a strange sight: a 'beheaded bubble.'

We can get bright colours, too, in the films formed in the square frame. To see them at their best they should be seen by reflected light i.e. you should be on the same side as the source of light; it is a good idea to have a dark screen behind the film.

A nest of bubbles

Wet the table top or, better, a black tray. Transfer a bubble from the funnel to the tray, making it into a big hemi-sphere. Dip a drinking straw into the soap solution, poke the straw through the bubble and gently blow a second bubble inside the first. Shake the bubble clear from the straw. We now have one bubble inside another.

36

30 A nest of bubbles

Next see if you can blow a third bubble inside the second. My record is four (see diagram 30): can you beat this?

An imprisoned frog

For this experiment you will need a saucer, a big funnel (e.g. 10 cm in diameter) fitted with a rubber tube and an object such as a plastic frog or doll small enough to fit under the funnel. Pour soap solution into the saucer. Stand the frog in the saucer. Cover the frog with the funnel. Blow gently down the tube, at the same time carefully lifting the funnel.

31 The imprisoned frog

When the bubble has reached a suitable size slowly turn the funnel onto its side, blowing gently all the time. With a shake, detach the bubble from the funnel. The frog will then be in the centre of the bubble: this frog will certainly not be able to go a-wooing. (See diagram 31).

Next crown the frog with a small bubble. To do this dip a straw into some soap solution. Push it through the bubble. Blow a small bubble on the end of the straw. With a little persuasion you should be able to get it to stay on the frog's head. Remove the straw to leave King Frog in sole possession.

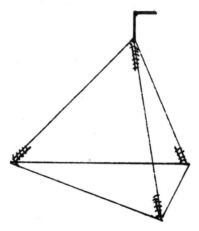

32   Tetrahedral frame

From spheres to cubes

(i) Make a tetrahedral frame-work with thick wires or thin knitting needles as in diagram 32. The tetrahedron has six edges and four sides. The wires are suitably bent at their ends and then fastened together at the corners by wrapping thin wire round them and then glueing. It does not matter if the joints are rather clumsy-looking. We are not interested in the corners of the frame.

The soap solution must now be made in a deeper vessel, e.g. a small bucket. Dip the frame into the bucket. When you take it out you should find four films meeting at the centre of the tetrahedron.

(ii) Next make a prismatic frame-work (see diagram 33). This has nine edges. By dipping it into the bucket you should be able to get an array of nine films.

38

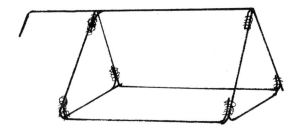

33   Prismatic frame

(iii) Finally make a cubical frame (see diagram 34). The first dip will probably produce eight films arranged around a central ninth film: this film looks rather like a window. Dip the frame-work a second time. With a little practise you will be able to get a cubical bubble at the centre. From spheres we have moved to cubes.

There are three maximum rules obeyed by these films:

the maximum number of $\left\{\begin{array}{l} \text{faces meeting along a common line is 3} \\ \text{faces meeting at a common point is 6} \\ \text{edges meeting at a common point is 4.} \end{array}\right.$

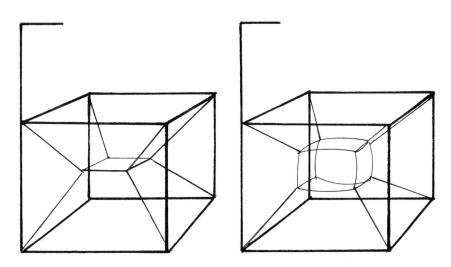

34   Cubical frame: first dip, second dip

39

Inside bottles

It is possible to fill bottles with bubbles. The bottles can be cylindrical like milk bottles or flat like medicine bottles.

Fill the bottle to the very top with solution. Wipe away any froth. Close the top with your fingers. Turn the bottle upside down and tilt it a little. Carefully move a finger to allow water to drip out and so let air bubbles gurgle their way in. You can arrange it so that the air bubbles are either small ones or big ones. When all the water has run away the bottle will be full of bubbles.

Stopper the bottle. Soon the bubbles will acquire attractive colours. The bubbles will last for days inside the bottle for here evaporation is restricted. After a time however, the bubbles become so thin that they lose their colours. They are then, indeed, very difficult to see except from the side.

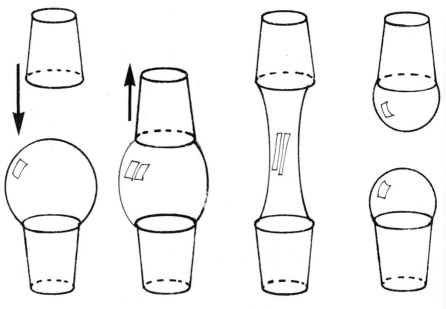

35   One bubble into two

Cylindrical bubbles

Transfer a bubble as before to a beaker. Bring down a second beaker (with wetted rim) onto the bubble. Lift this beaker up slowly (see diagram 35). The spherical bubble is pulled out, eventually becoming approximately cylindrical.

With further lifting of the top beaker the cylinder begins to go in at the middle — it acquires a waist. Soon it splits into two. Fission has taken place.

Fun with Mirrors

How big should a mirror be?

When you ask a friend how big a mirror should be for it to show the whole of your face, the answer quite often is that it depends upon how near the mirror is. This is not so however.

Measure the long side of a pocket mirror. Let us suppose that it is 3½ inches, a normal size. On a strip of paper stuck on your forehead mark off a line 7 inches above the end of your chin. You will find that if you hold the mirror at the correct angle you will be able to see from your chin end to the mark. A 3½ inch mirror shows 7 inches of face, just twice its length. This is true whether the mirror is near your face or at arm's length.

The missing gap

Place two pocket mirrors side by side on the table on a dark piece of paper. Look down at your face reflected in the mirrors and as you do so separate the mirrors so that there is a gap between them. You will still see the whole of your face. The gap which you might have expected will not be there. The reason for this is that we see with two eyes. If we look down with one eye closed then there will be a gap in the image of our face.

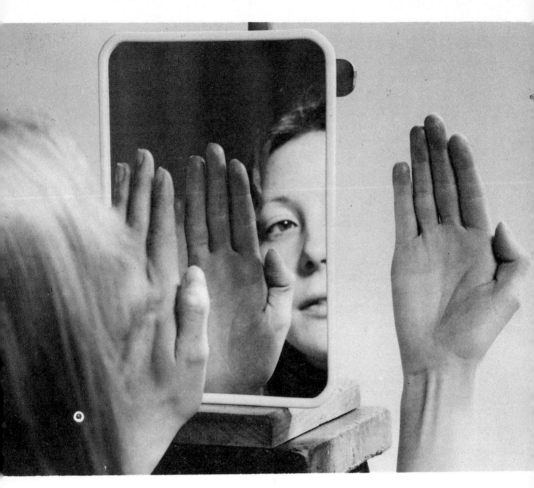

Two Right Hands!

The wrong way round

Hold your left hand up in front of a mirror. The image of your hand that you will see in the mirror is a right hand as the photo shows. The face that you look at in a mirror is not the face that your friends see, it is a wrong way round version of it. Write your first name on a piece of sticky paper and fix it on your forehead, then look at yourself in a mirror. The writing will be the wrong way round and therefore your face must be also.

Mirrors at right angles

As we have seen, the image formed by reflection from a mirror is the wrong way round. If we use not one mirror but two, thus having two reflections, the second reflection will give us an image which is the correct way round. We can put this in another way: the first reflection makes a right hand into a left one, the second reflection then turns this left hand back into a right one and so right has come out right in the end.

The two mirrors must be at right angles to each other. This can be arranged:

1) by cutting two slots at right angles to each other in a block of wood and then fitting the two mirrors into the slots

2) by glueing the two mirrors to each side of an angle bracket.

Hold the arrangement upright. Look at your right hand in it. Then look at your face in it (as in diagram 36). Wink one eye; stroke one side of your face; have your name, as before, on your forehead. You now see yourself as others see you.

36   Not you: you

Catching sunlight

You have probably already many times caught sunlight with a mirror and reflected it onto a distant wall. The delight in doing this is to see the speed with which the patch of light can be made to dance up and down.

The shape of this patch of light is worth observing. When the mirror is near to the wall on which the patch is being made, the shape of the patch is quite clearly the shape of the mirror; if the mirror is a rectangle the patch of light is a rectangle too. If the wall is further away the shape becomes less clear.

Cover a mirror so that only a 2 cm square of mirror is left. Let the sunlight reflected from this small square of mirror fall onto a wall 2 metres away. The patch will now be a circle, the shape of the sun. It will also be rather faint. Let it fall into a cardboard box whose sides (but not the end) have been blackened. The circular shape will now stand out more clearly.

A Magic Mirror?

Tell a friend that you have a magic mirror which can distinguish between red and yellow objects.

You need to make four cards, one half of each card being covered with yellow paper, the other half with red. With a felt-tipped pen, for example, draw black letters and figures on the cards as shown in diagram 37; the white half of the card in the diagram is to be red, the shaded half yellow.

Cards 1 and 2

In all four cases the mirror is placed upright on the table. Cards 1 and 2 in turn are placed flat on the table in front of the mirror. Look into the mirror. The letters L T V on the yellow background are turned upside down but B B C on red seems all right, that is, the right way up. Similarly 7 9 6 on yellow is upside down: 8 3 0 on red seems all right.

Of course it is all a trick. The letters B and C and the digits 0 3 and 8 have been used because they can be written so that they have an 'axis of symmetry' across their middle.

Other letters which can be used in this way are D E H I O X: the only other digit is I.

Cards 3 and 4

Before your friend has had time to 'tumble' to the trick, remove cards 1 and 2 and replace them in turn by cards 3 and 4 which are to be held up-right in front of the mirror.

| BBC | LTV |

| 830 | 796 |

| A
T
O
M | B
E
L
L |

| OTTO | GLEN |

37 Magic mirror

The ATOM on red appears unchanged, the BELL on yellow is turned round. The letters A T O and M have an axis of symmetry down their height: other such letters are H I U V W X and Y so altogether we have 11 letters to choose from. What is the longest vertical word you can make which will appear 'all right'?

A palindrome is a word like R A D A R or L E V E L which reads the same backwards as forwards. O T T O is a palindromic name which has been made out of two of the 11 letters given above. M U M, O X O and T U T - T U T are other words which could be used. Such words held up in front of a mirror will seem to be the right way round. What other words can you find?

Fun with Mechanics

Will it fall over?

For this experiment you need a long thin rod with a flat and smooth base. Wooden rods or cardboard tubes will do. To make the experiment impressive, the height of the rod should be at least 10 times its width. See if you can beat my record which is a height/width ratio of 20.

Stand the rod on a strip of paper near the edge of a smooth level table. Give the paper a quick jerk: with patience and practise you should be able to get the paper away and leave the rod still standing. If you cannot give a sharp enough jerk, try this: hold the strip away from the table. Bring the edge of a ruler down quickly onto the paper (diagram 38).

The paper when jerked moves with a very great momentary acceleration. To make the rod move with a big acceleration requires, because of its inertia, a big force. The frictional force between paper and rod is not great enough for this and so the rod stays put whilst the paper accelerates forwards.

If instead of jerking the paper strip you pull it gently and so give it only a small acceleration it will move forward with the paper and still stand upright. If you can maintain this steady, small acceleration you can make the rod move with quite a sizeable speed. When you stop pulling however, the rod will then topple forwards.

A pleasant variation of this experiment is to use, instead of a rod, a hammer standing on its head.

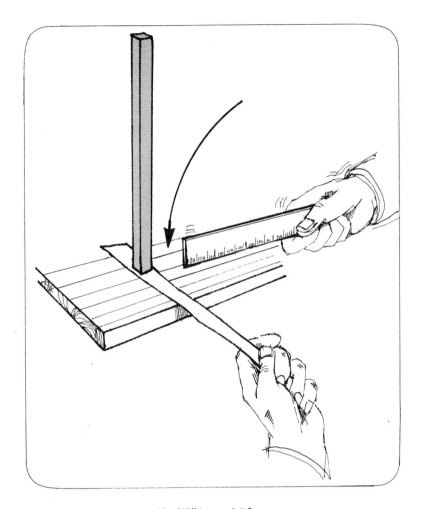

38 Will it, won't it?

Centres of gravity

i) The 'kelly', the doll that will not fall over, is well-known. It has a heavy spherical base. The top part has to be light in weight. In this way the centre of gravity is kept low. However much the kelly is tilted, its centre of gravity is moved higher than it was and so on being released it returns to its upright position.

47

plasticine

39　Home-made kelly

ii) Home-made kelly. Into a tin can pack, as shown in diagram 39, stones or old iron bolts etc. Fix them in position with glue or plasticine. As fancy suggests make a light headpiece or fix a long light rod. Push the kelly to one side. Provided the headpiece is light enough, the kelly will come back and after swinging to and fro return to the vertical position.

(iii) The trick stick. Fasten together two milk straws in line — the stick so made will be 30 cm long. Into one end fasten a steel drill, one that will just fit. The centre of gravity will now be well away from the middle of the stick, it may be only 6 cm from one end. The stick therefore will stay on the table even when there is a length of only 6 cm on the table. Somebody, not knowing that the stick is loaded, will be surprised to see it in this position and think that it is stuck to the table.

48

The straws are not opaque — the drill can just about be seen through the straw and so to make the trick more effective its presence must be concealed. This can be done by inserting a length of thin black paper at the other end so that the two ends look alike.

(iv) The stick on two fingers. Support a long uniform stick on two fingers as shown in diagram 40, finger A being nearer to one end. If you move A either inwards or outwards the stick does not move, A slips along it. But if you move B it takes the stick with it.

As B is nearer the centre of gravity it takes more of the weight of the rod than A does and so it has a firmer grip on the rod than A has.

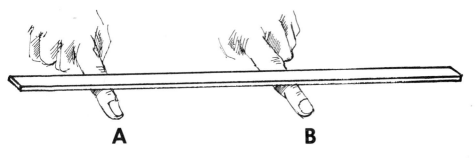

40   What will happen?

The swaying bird

This pleasant little toy can be made from scrap materials. A cork provides the centre piece (see photo). Two pins act as legs. A piece of cardboard, the neck and head, fits into a slot in the cork.

A stiff wire or thin needle, bent as shown, is pushed into the bottom end of the cork. A heavy body such as a steel bolt is fixed to the other end of the wire. (Block the centre of the bolt with wood and then bore a hole in the wood.)

Mount the bird on the edge of a table or on a ruler held horizontally. On being given a starting push it should swing gracefully to and fro before coming to rest. If it does not balance, re-shape the wire until it does.

The bird itself is very light (cork, cardboard and feather). The bolt is heavy. Thus the centre of gravity is near to the bolt. If it is below the feet of

49

the bird then the bird will stay balanced and, given a push, will swing to and fro.

There are many variations of this swaying bird: it can be a prancing horse or a curio from Africa (see diagram 41).

The swaying bird

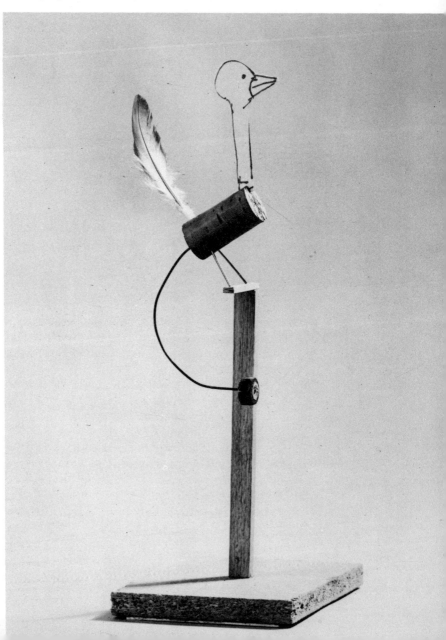

plasticine

41   African curio

42   Pulse magnifier

The pulse magnifier

We need a drawing pin with a spherical head, a little plasticine and a drinking straw. Cut the straw in two along its length: each half will serve as a very light pointer. Fix one of these pointers into the upturned pin as shown in diagram 42. We now have the movement magnifier. If it will not stay upright, cut pieces off the top until it will. It should be able to rock to and fro without toppling over. We have here indeed something like a kelly.

Look near your wrist for the pulsing point — if you cannot see it, feel for it with the forefinger of your other hand. When you have found the spot mark it with a pen. Then hold your arm out in a horizontal position. Put the magnifier on the marked spot. The pointer should then move backwards and forwards in a jerky way. The tip should move distances of about 1 cm.

If you have a stop-watch or a watch with a second hand you should be able to time your own pulse from the movement you see.

51

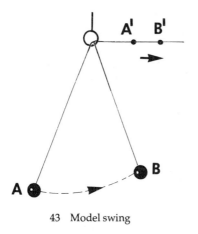

43 Model swing

How does a swing work?

We have all, when we were very young, delighted in the swings in the park. At first we were pushed by some kind adult. Then we learned the trick, really a very clever one, of 'working ourselves'. How can a child without touching the ground make herself go in ever bigger swings?

We can get some idea as follows. Hang a doll on a suitable length of string which at the top end is not fastened but passes over a hook or through a loop. The end of the string is held in the hand.

Give the doll a slight swing. As it swings from one side A to the other side B pull the string a little way from A^1 to B^1 (see diagram 43). This lifts up the doll so that B is higher than A. As the doll swings back from B to A let the string go back. Repeat this process, soon the doll will acquire big swings. You must take the time from the swing, it is no good trying to make the doll swing to your time.

Every time you pull on the string you are giving energy to the doll for you are lifting it up. This energy both keeps the doll swinging and makes the swings bigger ones.

A girl on a swing works herself by so moving her body that she is periodically raising and lowering her centre of gravity in time with the motion of the swing. To make the doll swing by pulling on the string it had to have a slight swing to begin with. The girl on the swing gives herself a start by pushing off with her feet from the ground or she asks somebody to start her off.

Newton's cradle

Newton's cradle

This toy when not in use is a handsome piece of furniture. Five steel balls hang from two horizontal rods as the photo shows. The balls must be lined up very carefully. Let us call the ball on the extreme left A, the next one B and so on to the fifth ball E.

(i) Pull A to the side, let it fall. It is brought to rest (very nearly) when it hits B. Ball E swings out. The motion of A, its 'momentum', has been transferred to E. When E swings back its momentum is transferred back to A and so the process is repeated. Gradually however the middle balls begin to swing and in the end all five balls swing together.

(ii) Swing 2, 3, 4 balls in turn. You will find that 2, 3 or 4 balls swing away.

(iii) Pull A and E away and release them at the same time. Each one swings back as if it was bouncing from the ball it hits. However if A is

53

pulled away only a small distance and E a big one, A rebounds with a big swing and E with only a little one. Thus A and E are exchanging their momenta.

(iv) With forefinger and thumb hold any one of the three inner balls still. Make A swing. When it collides with B, E will swing out even though the inner ball is being held.

The success of the toy depends upon and so illustrates the excellent elastic properties of steel. If the balls were made of lead the toy would not give much pleasure.

Five twopenny pieces can be used to show the transference of momentum. On a surface made as smooth as possible put the five coins touching each other in line. Move the first coin away but still in line. Flick it to make it collide head-on with the second coin. The coin at the far end moves away (see diagram 44).

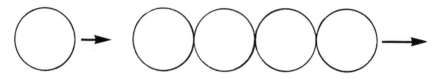

44   Five coins

The weightless moo-cow

Perhaps when you were much younger you played with the 'moo-cow' toy. You may think that nothing very scientific can be done with such a toy but if you do, you will be wrong for you can use it to show that important but difficult idea of 'weightlessness'. The toy is a cylinder about 6 cm long and 6 cm in diameter, with a perforated top.

Turned upside down nothing is heard. Turned back again it emits a noise which lasts two or three seconds. To me the noise sounds more like the bleating of a lamb than the mooing of a cow. If you shake it up and down you can make it quack like a goose.

Inside there is a bellows fitted with a mouthpiece. Turned upside down the heavy top of the bellows falls and the bellows fills with air. Turned back the bellows closes again, the heavy top pushing air out through the mouthpiece which is so shaped as to make a mooing noise.

Now try this: turn the moo-cow upside down and back again but as soon as it begins to moo let it drop. To avoid damage have a cushion in readiness to break its fall. The bigger the drop the more impressive the experiment. You will find that whilst falling the cow ceases to moo but having landed resumes and finishes its moo.

When falling the moo-cow is 'weightless'. The heavy top of the bellows accelerates downwards but so does the rest of the bellows and so no air is pushed out, no sound is heard.

One more thing to do: turn the moo-cow upside down, then back again and as soon as it begins to moo this time throw it upwards, making sure that the top part remains on top. Again no moo will be heard until the moo-cow has landed. On its *upward* journey the cow is accelerating *downwards*: it is weightless when going up just as when falling down.

Fun with Heat

This section is entitled Fun with Heat but as we are going to look at some experiments with ice it would be more accurate to describe it as Fun with Hot and Cold.

How warm is your hand?

Your family will probably receive official or business letters which have a transparent window through which the address can be read. Before we go on to the main use we are going to make of these windows cut one out and look through it at near and then distant objects. You will find that they are only transparent with very near objects; with distant ones they are opaque.

For the main experiment cut out a window — a typical size is 9 cm × 3 cm. Lay it on the palm of your hand. If your hand is warm, and hands generally are, the strip will rapidly curl up (see diagram 45). On my hand such a strip curls into a complete semi-circle in less than 4 seconds.

After you have used rectangular strips indulge your fancy and cut strips into such shapes as fishes, worms or eels, i.e. any long thin creature that you can expect to wriggle. You will find that the strips can be quite life-like in their behaviour.

Why does the strip curl like this? When one is placed on your hand the bottom side is warmed and so expands. The strip-material is a poor conductor of heat so the top side does not warm up and does not expand. Thus the strip curls so that the warm bottom side is on the outside, which is the longer side of the curve, and the cold top side is on the shorter inside.

45 Curling paper

For the strip to curve well it must be very thin and its material must be a good expander but a poor conductor of heat.

If the strip is licked with the warm tongue it curves even more quickly but when cooled and dried it does not recover its smoothness.

Creaking vessels

In the section on two-way floaters I mentioned the possibility of making a single vessel by glueing together two plastic tubs. With some oil paint round the common rim the combined vessel can be made air-tight.

Take such a vessel from a cold place to a hot one: you may hear a sharp crack or a series of creaks. These noises are also to be heard if the vessel is taken from a hot place to a cold one. When the air inside the vessel warms up its pressure increases and this increase may be great enough to make part of the tub bulge outwards. Similarly if the air cools down its pressure decreases and then the external atmospheric pressure may make the tub bulge inwards.

You may not succeed in getting such a creaking vessel the first time you glue two plastic tubs together. If you don't, try a different type of tub next time. Some tubs show the effect more markedly than others.

The expansion-contraction of air with change of temperature is made use of in the hot-air engine.

Model Hot Air Engines

Model *steam* engines are very popular. At the beginning of this century model *hot-air* engines were quite common. As they were made of solid materials you may still be able to pick one up in a second-hand or antique shop. They were even used for doing simple jobs such as working fans, but electric motors soon replaced them.

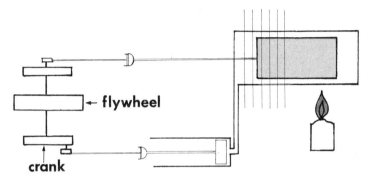

46   Hot Air engine

Diagram 46 will help to explain the working of a 19th century German hot air engine. There are two cylinders. The right hand end of the bigger cylinder is heated by a spirit lamp: the other end is cooled by the fins which surround it.

Inside this cylinder is a loose-fitting piston. When this piston is at the left-hand end of the cylinder the air in the cylinder is then heated by the lamp and so expands. Some of it slips past the piston, along a connecting tube and into the smaller cylinder.

This second cylinder is fitted with a close-fitting piston which is pushed outwards by the expanding air. The piston works a crank which turns the flywheel. The flywheel in its turn works a second crank which pushes the displacer piston back to the right hand end of its cylinder. The air is now in the cool end of the cylinder and so contracts. This causes air to leave the smaller cylinder so that the atmospheric pressure will now push its piston inwards.

Thus a cycle of changes has been completed; we are back where we started and the engine can keep on working. The expansion-contraction of the air causes the piston to move to and fro: this 'reciprocating' motion causes the flywheel to go round and round.

57

The disadvantage of a model steam hot-air engine is that it has very little power. The advantages are:

it will start, given a push, after only twenty seconds

there is no danger of an explosion

unlike a steam engine which eventually runs out of water it never runs out of air.

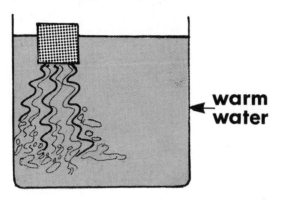

warm water

47   Cold water current

Ice-cubes

(i) Drop an ice-cube onto warm water in a transparent vessel, one at least 6 inches deep. The ice-cube floats of course. Look at the underneath of the floating ice-block. You will see a downward current of what looks like an oily liquid (diagram 47). It is, however, only ice-cold water which sinks through the less-dense warm water. The oily appearance is due to the warm and cold water refracting light by different amounts.

If the ice-cubes are made from water which has been coloured by a drop of ink, the current of cold water sinking down shows up more clearly.

(ii) Press two ice-cubes together and then relax the pressure. Generally, if the pressure was great enough, the ice-cubes will stay stuck together as a single cube.

Ice under pressure melts so when the two cubes are pressed together they melt at those places where they touch. When the pressure is no longer exerted freezing-up again occurs.

Snowballs, as we all know, are made by pressing snow-flakes together. Where the flakes touch, the pressure is great and melting occurs. When the pressure is taken off, freezing up occurs and the flakes are now stuck together by ice. That is why a snowball makes so effective a missile.

58

But it's still whole!

(iii) A thin wire under tension wrapped round a block of ice will pass through the ice but the block will still be a single one at the end.

The usual size of ice-cube ($2 \times 2\frac{1}{2} \times 3$ cm) is just a little small for this experiment so instead I make rather bigger ice-blocks. For this purpose I use the rectangular lids of the boxes in which some makes of colour slides are stored. If you do not have such a lid you can make a cardboard box, about $8 \times 2 \times 2$ cm, and line it with polythene sheet.

Thin copper wire is required. Only short lengths are needed so perhaps a friendly science teacher will let you have some. Suitable gauges are 32, 34 or 36. The wire must be bare. If it is enamelled then the enamelling must be removed. This can be done by means of fine sand-paper. The 36 gauge wire will take a load of 1 lb or $\frac{1}{2}$ kilogram: the 32 gauge, 2 lbs or 1 kg.

The frame-work shown in the photo is helpful for holding the ice-block but you can simply use tin cans. The cross-piece at the top is in two parts

59

with a gap in the middle. A lump of plasticine at the base will catch the weight when it has worked its way through the block. The weight is held up by a rubber band. The wire is curled round and fastened to this band.

The ice-block is put in place and the load is suspended from the block. In a time of about 3 minutes the wire will have melted its way through the block and yet the block is still whole.

I have cut in this way through an ice-block as many as 20 times.

The drinking duck

We all know that wet clothes are cold clothes. When water evaporates, as it does from the wet clothes, it cools. This is basically how the 'drinking duck' works.

The flannel head of the duck is pushed down into the water in the beaker until it is well and truly wet. On being let go it will then swing to and fro, gradually tilting forwards, getting nearer to the water. Eventually it topples over, has another drink, springs back and so the whole process is continually repeated. A typical time between drinks is 20 seconds. The duck will continue to swing and drink for many hours. This is not however perpetual motion, for eventually the water in the beaker will dry up and then the duck will come to rest.

Diagram 48 will help you to understand how the duck works. It contains a liquid such as methyl chloride which is near its boiling point at ordinary temperatures. The space above the liquid is filled with vapour. As the head of the duck is wet it is therefore cold. This causes the vapour here to condense, which lowers the pressure in the head. Liquid is then forced up the central tube and so the duck becomes top-heavy. When it topples over, the liquid which has been forced up into the head is able to return to the base and so the whole process repeats.

On dry days or in draughty places the rate of evaporation from the wet head increases and so the duck drinks more frequently. It is amusing to see what happens when the beaker of water is removed from the thirsty duck. Provided the tilt of the stand is just right, the duck, disappointed at not finding water where it should be, topples right over, ending with its bottom in the air.

A word of caution: the toy is perfectly safe if not broken. The liquid inside it may be unpleasant to breathe and may be inflammable. The toy should therefore not be knocked about violently and so should be kept away from young children.

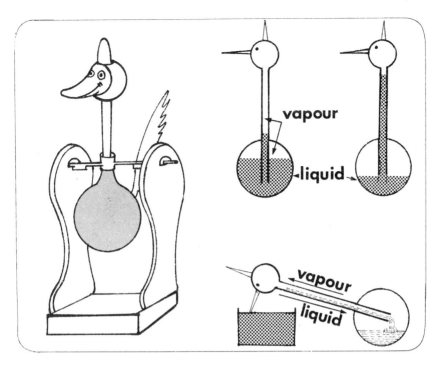

48 The drinking duck

Fun with Magnetism and Electricity

Magnetic compasses

Steel objects such as paper clips and sewing needles when stroked with a powerful magnet become magnetised themselves. If they are free to rotate they will then set themselves approximately N and S. In Britain magnetic N is a little to the west of true geographic N.

As we have already seen paper clips can be floated on water — if they are magnetised they will then set themselves N and S. One paper clip by itself will give N and S. Two floating clips will show mutual attraction or repulsion.

A magnetic compass can be made from a press-stud, two small needles and a pin. Cut out a piece of card 2 cm by 1 cm. Make a hole in its centre.

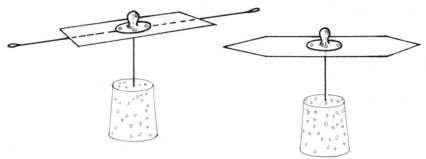

49   Compasses, magnetic, electrostatic

As shown in diagram 49 glue to it the top half, the dome, of a press-stud (such studs, also called snap fasteners, are sold by drapers). Glue two needles to the bottom side of the card. The pin is mounted point upwards in a cork. The dome of the press-stud is then placed on this pin: this provides a frictionless bearing for the magnetic compass.

Electrostatic compasses

Again we use a press-stud and pin to provide the bearing. The press-stud is glued to a piece of cardboard shaped as shown in diagram 49. Disused detergent bottles if dry become strongly charged with electricity when rubbed by a flannel duster or nylon sheet. From the charged bottle electrostatic field lines spread out. The electrostatic compass sets itself along these field lines just as iron filings set themselves along magnetic field lines.

See from how big a distance you can make the charged bottle control the electrostatic compass.

Flying saucers

First set up the arrangement shown in the photo. A tin can is fastened either by glue or screw to an upturned plastic carton — such cartons are good insulators. The carton in its turn is fastened to a suitable base. Tissue paper or thin paper circles are cut out or punched out. These are to be the flying saucers.

One is placed on the rim of the tin. A detergent bottle is charged by friction and then put into the can. The can now becomes electrified and so does the paper circle. Like charges repel and so the circle being of small weight jumps off. See how far you can make it jump. Other good jumpers are such things as thistledown or dandelion parachutes.

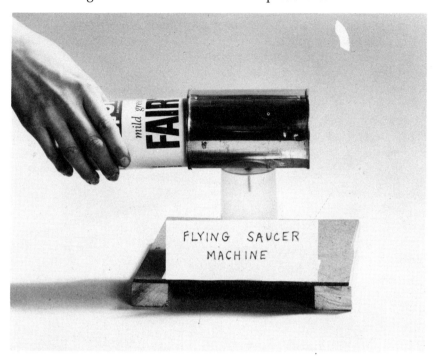

Flying saucers

Radio Rex

We will end Fun with Physics with a description of Radio Rex, a scientific toy made in the 1920s. Such toys are not on sale today and they are not very easy to make. Perhaps this account of the toy will stimulate you to make a modern transistorised version.

In the photo Radio Rex, a plastic bulldog 3 cm tall and 4 cm long, stands in the doorway of his kennel, as fierce a plastic bulldog as one ever saw. I push him into his kennel so that he is out of sight. I shout CATS and out he jumps at great speed from the depths of the kennel. Of course he will also jump out if I shout DOGS or indeed if I bang the table.

63

Inside the kennel there is a 1½ volt cell and an electromagnet. When Rex is pushed in, he, in his turn, pushes an iron strip so that it completes a circuit. This brings the electromagnet into action: it is powerful enough to hold the iron spring in position.

On the side of the kennel, as the photo shows, there hangs a piece of brass which gently touches two wires on the side of the kennel. The current flows in from one wire, across the brass and out through the other. Any vibration, such as a sound wave, if it is big enough, on passing the brass will disturb it and so for a moment break the circuit. The electromagnet is thus put out of action, the iron spring is released and shoots Rex out of his kennel. A modern version of Rex will use in place of the hanging brass a microphone which can be much more sensitive. A mere *whisper* of 'cats' should now bring out the fiery bulldog.

Radio Rex